REFINED BY FIRE

The Practical Principles of Passionate Leadership

Randy Fox

Copyright © 2014 by Randy Fox, FoxPoint LLC

Refined by Fire

All rights reserved. This book or any portion thereof may not be reproduced or used in any manner whatsoever without the express written permission of the publisher except for the use of brief quotations in a book review.

ISBN 978-0-9914669-1-7

Printed in the United States of America

First Edition, 2014

Second Edition, 2016

REFINED BY FIRE

Practical Principles of Passionate Leadership

Refined by Fire

CHAPTER 1	Priority Number One	1
CHAPTER 2	The Career for You	17
CHAPTER 3	Managing Your Ego	25
CHAPTER 4	Honing Your Skills	37
CHAPTER 5	Your Work Ethic	47
CHAPTER 6	Advisers	55
CHAPTER 7	Using Failure to Succeed	65

Refined by Fire

DEDICATION

*To my three children,
Trevor, Brendon and Nevaeh;
your journey is my journey,
may you always remember
to be refined by His fire.*

PROLOGUE

The Importance of Refinement

> "Look around you. Everything changes. Everything on this earth is in a continuous state of evolving, refining, improving, adapting, enhancing, ...changing. You were not put on this earth to remain stagnant."
> — Steve Maraboli

Yeah, look around you.

If you want to make an impact on the world in the 21st Century, it's time to get to work. It's time to turn your dreams into reality.

How do you reach your potential?

By experiencing it.

Life is not a stream of consciousness, it's a struggle. Making it of value and fulfilling is the hardest thing you will ever do. It's not for the fainthearted or the frivolous. It's for those who are willing to go through the fire and come out stronger on the other side.

There are three types of people: those that run from the fire, those that are consumed by it and those who are refined by it.

The fire is not for the fearful but for the fearless. It is the fire that is made of hellish components, failures, setbacks, confusion, doubts, tragedies, uncertainty, suffering and sadness.

It is the fire of life.

It is the fire that separates the dreamers from the doers. It is the fire that determines what your life can be and will become.

Or not.

Like gold refined by fire, you will become more valuable as you forge ahead through the blast furnace towards your ultimate success, towards the leader you were destined to become in life.

The words you will be absorbing in these pages were created to enable you to welcome that fire, not walk away from it. It is necessary you enter these flames or you will never realize the depth, the texture or the power you can experience as a human being.

That is the nature of refinement.

Refine: def. To enlarge or improve (upon) by making subtle or fine distinctions, to bring to a finer state or form by purifying.

The more gold is refined by fire, the more valuable it becomes. The more you stay and face life with all its powerful forces, the greater the leader you will become.

Soul on Fire challenged you to follow your Impossible Dream. It's a book of inspiration.

Refined by Fire is a book of instructions.

Practical Principles of Passionate Leadership.

The Gold Standard of a Life Worth Living You are that Standard.

My book cover is your constant reminder of what you were meant to be; passionate, powerful and 99.99% leadership pure.

Refining Gold

The final stage of gold production – refining – involves removing impurities that remain after the smelting process. Refining companies receive Doré bars, as well as scrap gold, and re-liquefy the metal in a furnace.

Workers add borax and soda ash to the molten metal, which separates the pure gold from other precious and less precious metals.

A sample is then taken to a lab for tests, or assays, that measure the gold content. In most cases, the gold is 99.99 percent pure. Workers cast the gold produced during refining into bars.

Refined by Fire is the literary form of building you into that valuable commodity. We will supply you with the borax and soda, the practical steps necessary to add expertise to your endeavors.

We will walk with you through the practical aspects of the "furnace process" and your career passions, to show how you can use heat and fire to reach the top of your profession.

Many organizations tend to be like a stagnant church, **"*exhortation without explanation.*"**

That is not the purpose of my challenge to you.

This book is about the nitty-gritty *how-to* refine your life at any age. It is on how to use the fire to your advantage.

On how to consistently become a better leader.

"If you wish to achieve worthwhile things in your personal and career life, you must become a worthwhile person in your own self-development."
Brian Tracy

The self-development outlined in these pages will include your priorities, how you manage your time, your ego, your relationships, your work ethic, your skills and more.

I believe my life is the most important thing I do. My dream is to work on making mine the best it can be, *and* to suggest practical steps to give you that same experience, too.

Albert Einstein stated, "Only a life lived for others is a life worthwhile."

Life is out there waiting for you to attack it confidently in a renewed way. You will need passion, purpose, an open-mind, decisiveness, humility, a risk-taking attitude and a strong work ethic.

Great skills and talent aren't enough. Your greatness isn't dependent on expertise alone, but on enthusiasm, drive and your determination to improve.

I will supply the practical insights. Let's work together to achieve that truism of your success: "As you improve, your career will expand."

You will be **Refined by Fire**.

Are you ready?

The world is waiting for you!

CHAPTER ONE

PRIORITY NUMBER ONE

Before we begin, let's make one thing clear:

"No matter how many personal productivity techniques you master, there will always be more to do than you can ever accomplish in the time you have available...no matter how much it is."
Brian Tracy

Now, we understand there is no magic formula for prioritization or for creating more time. Let's do the best we can to be the best we can be.

PRIORITY: def. a thing that is regarded as more important than another.

You notice this is not just defined as more important than something else; it is something *you* regard as more important. The key to your priority list falls upon you. Therefore, your priorities are you. So think hard...what do you value most. Make a list that includes three to five values. You cannot truly value ten or twenty things.

"We do what we really want to do."

So, there are two considerations when it comes to successful prioritization. The first is being wise in the selection process and the second is to put them in order.

I call this your *Career Value System.*

CAREER VALUE SYSTEM: def. the system of established values, norms, or goals existing in your career and life.

Every successful individual has operated from their career value system to fulfill their passionate dream in life. This system was their career base camp as they peered up at Everest.

Here are several practical truths about your career value system:

It needs to be your heart

Before you order your priorities, take time to search your soul. If you're going to run the race of your life, make certain you are putting your life's passions in the starting blocks. Don't think of your priorities as a job description. They're the foundation of all the dreams you want to come true, both daily and forever.

It needs to be optimistic, organized & operable

I want you to be excited and positive about your career value system. Setting down your priorities is an upbeat proposition. Organize them in the order of their importance to you and make certain they are realistic enough to be operable. This is not a set of theories; this is a system of *action.*

It needs to be adapted from time to time

As your life and career change, your value system

needs to flex with it. Keep tweaking it as you grow. Stay a step ahead of the rat race and you will never become a hamster on a wheel. In the movie, *The Graduate,* Ben was advised to remember one word, "plastics." Here is your word, "proactive." Stay on top of your game.

It needs to provide the proper balance for the tentacles of your life

Your career value system should be designed to streamline your life, not sabotage it. It's not a set of rules that stifles your success; it's a clarified set of sound principles that balances it. When you don't have a balanced foundation to succeed, you won't. Your system is there to keep your work and home life in its proper perspective.

It needs to be your ongoing wake-up call

Think of your value system as an advanced GPS tool. If you stray off course, it's there to remind you that you need to adjust your steering and get back on the road before you lose your way. If any of your secondary priorities begin to take over your life, there could be problems for you.

"Recalculating. Recalculating. Recalculating."

Time for the rubber to meet the road. It's time to build your career value system.

1. Simply list your priorities

   Begin by making a general list of your career values which *may* include: words or phrases, family, work, salary and bonus, co-workers, clients, health and exercise, finances, weekly goals, future projections, church, house, asset management, etc.

2. Put your priority list in order of importance

   This is critical for you. Make certain your values are prioritized. In life you may be faced with two good things at the same time. By having priorities and placed in order you will know which one to turn to first.

3. Make specific goals under your general topics

   For example, under family you will set specific goals for your marriage, your child's well-being, spending time together, vacations, etc. Do this with each category. The specifics are up to you.

4. Review your career value system list and *own* it

   Why? This is an important investment for your life. Make the investment count. If you do things the same way as before, you'll get the same results.

   You're looking for new, improved results for your exciting future. Spend time working your system. Remember:

   "All roads lead somewhere, it just depends on where you want to go!"

   Use your Career Value System as your guide to present day and future dreams. Stay with it.

> **"Decide what you want,
> decide what you are willing to exchange for it.
> Establish your priorities and go to work."**
> H. L. Hunt

Now that you've mapped out your *Career Value System,* let's drill down to living it out in a practical way.

I call this your *Short-Term Value System*.

1. Generally list your daily, weekly and monthly priorities

   Make a general list of all the things you want to accomplish in the next thirty (30) days.

2. Separate your goals into daily, weekly and monthly segments

3. Organize your goals in priority order beginning with your monthly list and working backwards

   Set your future projections first since you will be more focused that day on your daily list.

4. Organize your *daily* priorities in order of importance for each day

   I ask myself, "What are most important things that I want to accomplish today?" To help accomplish my list, I schedule a meeting with *myself* from 4:00–5:00 p.m. to review my progress. That is my private time to make any changes in my performance.

5. Do number one first

   Regardless of complexity, set a priority, and accomplish number one first. The trajectory of your day depends on performance and the positive effect of taking care of priority number one will create a momentum of success.

6. When #1 is done you work on the new #1

   One by one, knock down your daily priority list. As you approach each new goal ask yourself, "Is this negotiable or unnecessary?" If so, cross it off and move on to the next item.

7. Take breaks throughout the day

   Call your spouse or relationship partner, call a friend, get up and walk around inside or outside, go to lunch away from your desk, lean back in your chair and close your eyes for five minutes, talk to a co-worker for a few minutes, let your brain rest and breathe. Then, come back and hit the next item on your list.

8. Get home for dinner every night

   Your family is waiting for you. They're most likely Priority #1 in your life and for each day. Make sure you give them the "first piece of your cake daily, not just the crumbs."

9. Leave your business conversations at the office

   Sometimes this cannot be helped. Understandable. Do your best to disconnect from work, including your smart phone. Enjoy your family, they need your full presence, love and attention.

10. Adjust your daily list as you go

    Don't fall into the trap of "The Messiah Complex," where you begin to believe you are the only one that can fix everything. Just do your best and contribute daily. You'll soon figure out what you can and cannot realistically accomplish in your day. If that means you come in an hour earlier to fix it, so be it. It's better to leave earlier in the morning than to come home an hour late for dinner, or to miss your child's event.

> **"Besides the noble art of getting things done, there is the noble art of leaving things undone. The wisdom of life consists in the elimination of nonessentials."** Lin Yu Tang

You've set your plan, now what you are chasing?

There is a great movie line in the film, *My Best Friend's Wedding*. It's during the chase scene when the Julia Roberts character (Julianne) is following the fiancé of Cameron Diaz (Michael) in the hopes of catching him and changing his choice of marriage partners from Ms. Diaz (Kimmy) to *her*.

George Downes, the man sitting next to Julianne, sardonically asks several questions pointing out the futility of her pursuing Kimmy's love, Michael.

Here's the dialogue:

George Downes: Michael's chasing Kimmy?

Julianne Potter: Yes!

George Downes: You're chasing Michael?

Julianne Potter: YES!

George Downes: Who's chasing you...nobody, get it? There's your answer. It's Kimmy."

In other words, the Julia Roberts character, which is in love with Michael, is wasting her time because he's not in love with *her*, but with Kimmy.

The message in the movie to Julianne is that her priority is misguided, hopeless and a waste of time. She is hell bent on marrying Michael who is in love with another woman.

She needs to change her priority ASAP. The way she does that is simple.

She stops the car and ends the worthless pursuit.

There is a lesson for all of us here. We begin with the question, "What are you *chasing*?"

It's important that when you set your priorities, ensure your goals are realistic, noble, and reflect your value system.

If not, you may be spending every day of your career wasting time and energy.

> **"It's not so much how busy you are, but why you are busy. The bee is praised. The mosquito is swatted."**
> Mary O'Connor

The beginning of a passionate list of priorities is your soul's goal. You have to be clear in your heart what you're doing and ***why*** you're doing it.

The legendary football coach, Vince Lombardi always had a short, but powerful list of priorities for his players:

God

Your family

The Green Bay Packers

He set it in motion and whenever one of his players deviated from that list, Coach Lombardi would not so gently help him get back on track.

In this crazy age of social media, fast responses to everything, instant need for information and gratification, loyalty programs, email marketing and more...we need to stop the madness.

Try this.

Opt out of everything, and I mean everything. Unsubscribe from emails, discontinue magazine subscriptions, clear your calendar and start over.

Then, opt back in to only those things that truly matter and fit your priorities in life. You will be amazed how much more time you have and the wonderful joy and fulfillment that will come in leading a life focused on what matters to you most.

It's time for you to make your list, or for many of you, to refresh your list of priorities. Maybe your original list was great for a time in your career, but things have changed for you.

Time to adjust it.

Make sure you know what you are *chasing* and if that is truly what you should be pursuing in your life.

> **"Rowing harder doesn't help
> if you're headed
> in the wrong direction."**
> Bernajoy Vaal

One of the simple mistakes we make with priorities is our willingness to shuck them when a new situation arises.

Case in point.

You are about to have a critical meeting with an important client and just before you walk in the door you receive an email from the home office with a situation that requires your attention.

You stop in the hallway and read the message and as a result, the issue at the office is on your mind during your entire conversation. You are distracted, not engaged with the client and ultimately, not effective in your presentation.

Here is the concept to learn from this example:

"Whatever you do, wherever you are, always be fully present and engaged."

That means you resist the temptation to open your email and wait until after your meeting with the client. This keeps you completely present, focused and *in the moment* with your customer.

When you are with someone, whether it be your client, a co-worker, your boss, your wife or anyone else, learn to give them your complete attention during that time.

Because, at that moment, they're your #1 priority. If your mind is elsewhere it's like having one foot on the dock and one foot in the boat. You will be off balance and in danger of going under.

Answer the email later. It can wait.

> "You must live in the present,
> launch yourself on every wave,
> and find your eternity in each moment."
> Henry David Thoreau

You need to prioritize your activities. For example, you may be talented in several areas but that doesn't mean you should spend your time in any of those areas.

At a recent conference, Kip was in charge of the program. It included food and beverages for the luncheon. He made a decision to save a little money and stage a barbecue.

So far, so good.

Then, his priority list for his conference got away from him. Kip wound up in the local grocery store asking to speak to an assistant manager. When the supervisor arrived Kip introduced himself, "I'm Kip Klein and I need to buy 600 hamburger buns."

Huh?

Why is Kip Klein at the grocery store when he is in charge of the overall conference?

Because, he is a control freak.

He doesn't trust another person to purchase the right brand of hamburger buns. On his jaunt to the supermarket he also bought pickles, onions, condiments, three types of cheeses, chips, dips, sodas, coffee and water.

What a waste of his time and talent.

The moral of this story is simple: Learn to delegate.

Or else.

> "A leader should be in charge
> of the overall direction of a team.
> He is the one looking ahead,
> steering the course and making needed
> corrections to avoid getting off track.
> But buried in the small details,
> a man will lose the big picture and fail to see
> that the mission
> is falling apart until it is too late."
> — Brett & Kate McKay

I love the quarterback because they are in charge of their destiny. If they hesitate, they get sacked and thrown for a loss. If they call the wrong plays their team will have to punt. If they make a wrong decision on a pass, they get intercepted and lose the ball.

But, if they are wise, decisive, consistently make good plays and stick to their game plan, they have a great chance to score continuously and win the game.

So do you.

Be the quarterback. Don't let someone else dictate your priorities in life. Believe in your Career Value System and work it or you will lose the power of it being effective for you.

> "Decide what your priorities are
> and how much time you'll spend on them.
> If you don't someone else will."
> — Harvey Mackay

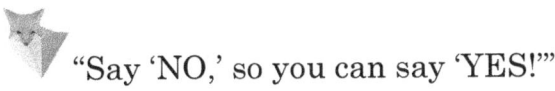 "Say 'NO,' so you can say 'YES!'"

**"I learned that we can do anything,
but we can't do everything...
at least not at the same time.
So think of your priorities not in terms of what
activities you do, but when you do them.
Timing is everything."** Dan Millman

In 1998, I was in my 14th season as an amateur baseball umpire. I was being encouraged by the pros to go to Florida and try out for the big leagues.

I was also a basketball referee and I had an ambition to rise in the collegiate game, as well. I had to decide between the two sports.

I was at a crossroads.

I had a full time job, a wife and a newborn child at home. We had just been relocated to a new town. There was a lot going on in my life. I was not able to commit the time, energy and focus required with everything that was in my life and be great at them all.

Something had to go.

Priorities needed to be made. I needed to invest in what was most important to me. My family and my career came first, those areas were locked in.

The choice was baseball or basketball. I knew that both weren't an option.

I chose basketball. I made it a priority. Saying no to one thing and making another a priority was the key for me here. It was the right decision for me.

The ability to focus helped me to improve and enjoy basketball. So much so, it has become an integral part of my life, and my business.

I'm honored to work in multiple leagues, including at the Division I level. I'm a Coordinator of Officials in multiple NCAA conferences, and I collaborate with two other wonderful friends to host an officiating development camp each summer for nearly 100 officials.

None of this would have come to fruition without the ability to make a key priority decision nearly 20 years ago.

> "To comprehend a man's life,
> it is necessary to know not merely what he does but also what he purposely leaves undone.
> There is a limit to the work that can be got out of a human body or a human brain, and he is a wise man who wastes no energy on pursuits for which he is not fitted;
> and he is still wiser who,
> from among the things he can do well, chooses and resolutely follows the best."
> William Gladstone

Just a final reminder.

You have a family. However big or small, close or far away, they need you. If you're married, especially if you have children; they are not your career, they are your life. Making money and providing for them is essential but it is not enough.

"Your family needs more than your monthly paycheck, they need *you*."

Never forget that.

If you are going to err on the side of working too much and not being there for them or working less and being the love of their lives, I have a strong suggestion for you.

Work less.

Your moments without them can never be redeemed. Your memories with them can never be removed.

They are your first priority. Everything else is a distant second.

Your *Career Value System* is your toolbox. Actually, I think we'll change the name…your *Life Value System*, is your best solution.

Your family is your treasure. Make sure you love them every day. Make sure they know you do.

> **"Spend time with those you love.
> One of these days you will say either,
> 'I wish I had,' or 'I'm glad I did.'"**
> Zig Ziglar

Believe it.

CHAPTER TWO

THE CAREER FOR YOU

All his life, Daniel had been imaginative, a dreamer. He never quite fit in at school, in class or on the playground. He never had a savings account and as soon as he made money, he spent it or reinvested it.

When he played *Monopoly*, as a kid, he would immediately gobble up every property he landed on. He didn't care if he won or lost or had a lot of money. He just loved the action of the score.

He was definitely an "outside the box" young man.

Upon graduation from college, Daniel accepted a position with a bank and quickly made his way up the corporate ladder to branch manager. The financial institution he worked for had big plans for him. It would not be long until Daniel would become a senior Vice-President or even higher in the business.

There was only one problem.

Daniel was miserable.

He hated his job. He hated every new promotion. He even hated all the money he was making.

Why?

Daniel was not a banker.

He was a thoroughbred, not a plow horse. He belonged on a race track not in a furrowed field. He was a power guy, not a policy manager.

His talents, tendencies and passion were better suited for a different career. He needed one that set him free to express and expand his talents beyond the bank site; which was serving as his professional prison.

He worked one more year while he built a base for his own business. Daniel began his own real estate development company. Now, he was free to come and go as he pleased and create his own Monopoly game, with his rules.

Daniel had accomplished the dream of every man or woman who has ever worked for a living. He had found the Gold Standard for his life.

Are you ready to establish yours?

> "For many, a job is more than income; it's an important part of who we are. So, a career transition of any sort is one of the most unsettling experiences you can face in your life."
> Paul Clitheroe

And, in Daniel's case, a necessary one.

This may be true in your career, as well.

It is critical that you figure out who you are and where you place yourself in the career world. Don't meander from interview to interview.

Be purposeful in your understanding of what you do best and precise in your selection of where to express it as a vocation.

It may be the perfect time for you to make your transition to personal greatness.

No matter your age or experience, here is an innovative way to determine a career that is perfect for you.

Step One

Take a blank page of paper and draw a vertical line three quarters of the way down the middle of it.

Step Two

On the left hand side write down what you would love to do with your day if someone subsidized you for $100,000 to take every day off for a year. What would you do every day with your free time if you didn't have to work?

Just list your favorite pastimes, hobbies and activities you enjoy the most. These may include, working in the garage, fixing your car, designing your home, talking on the phone, watching television, going to sporting events, volunteering at a charity, etc.

Step Three

On the right hand side list the compliments you have heard regarding your assets, skills or abilities, such as: "You're a great sales person," "You have an eye for art," "You inspire people," "You're really funny!" or, "You're a great cook!"

Step Four

On the bottom ¼ of the page, take concepts from the left column and mix them with compliments from the right hand column. Now, list potential careers at the bottom of your sheet that fit your favorite activities, along with those compliments.

For example, I have always enjoyed socializing with others; I'm a people-person. I love training people in the business world and I am told I have a gift for inspiring others. What career would fit these combinations?

A professional speaker, of course!

Welcome to my world.

My passion for this career was always inside me, but for the past twenty years, instead of having the calling of my heart, I toiled away in the corporate world. Now, I am fired up to work and be great at what I enjoy most!

> "Choose a job you love, and you will never have to work a day in your life."
> Confucius

Here are how-to's on defining your job niche even further. Take out another sheet of paper or open a new Word file and answer these questions (choose either A or B for each set of questions):

A. Do you like working with things (computers, construction, numbers, etc.)?

B. Do you like working with people?

A. Do you prefer to work within a group setting?
B. Do you prefer to always lead the group?

A. Do you tend to be analytical and detailed?
B. Do you tend to be conceptual and "Big Picture" oriented?

A. Do you tend to save every penny?
B. Do you see money as a means to an end?

A. Are you more comfortable being a follower?
B. Do you prefer to be the leader?

A. Do you prefer to be under a boss?
B. Would you rather be your own boss?

A. Do you like the security of a set weekly paycheck?
B. Do you want the freedom to make as much (or little) money per month?

A. Do you enjoy coming to work and going home at the same time each day?
B. Do you want to set your own hours and days when you work?

A. Do you prefer working inside?
B. Are you an outdoors person?

A. Are you left-brained?
B. Are you right-brained?

A. Do you have problems with rejection or criticism from others?
B. Are you thick skinned?

A. Are you a status quo person?
B. Are you a rebel?

These questions will get you started...

> **"To find a career to which you are adapted by nature, and then to work hard at it is about as near to a formula for success and happiness as the world provides."**
> Mark Sullivan

If you answered, "A" to most of the questions, you tend to be a status quo individual who likes security, plays it safe and sees a career as a steady job.

If you answered, "B" to most of the questions, you are the entrepreneurial type, a risk taker, a dreamer and a person who wants total control of your destiny, not entrusting it to a company or a corporation.

Neither A or B is better than the other. The importance here is which letter best defines your work preferences. This is a survey not a final exam.

The important thing here is to find your niche. When you do, you will thrive more than you ever have in life.

I labored in the corporate trenches for two decades and it enabled me to build a nice career and a financially stable portfolio. I was able to provide for my family and we never struggled with bills or debts.

Now, don't get me wrong, all of those experiences, successes and failures prepared me for today. I wouldn't trade the foundation I was given. I certainly wouldn't trade the memories and the great friends I have today from those years.

But, I always knew I was meant for something beyond pleasing corporate management. My soul cried out for challenges and expressions that were over the next mountain.

Recalling the experience reminds me of a line from one of my favorite books; *Who Moved My Cheese,* where Spencer Johnson asks us:

"What would you do if you weren't afraid?"

It wasn't time for me to play safe, it was time for me to soar. I spread my wings and began writing and speaking and consulting and I felt a sense of exhilaration I had never experienced in my life.

Did my cash flow take a hit?

For a while, yes.

Were there nights when I laid in bed and worried about my future and the future of my family?

A few.

Did I make the right move for the sake of my passionate purpose in life?

Absolutely.

Simply put, you cannot be afraid to dream, to jump, to make the move and live the life that you were born to live.

You may be doing good things but as Voltaire succinctly stated, "The best is the enemy of the good."

And, you deserve the best. Always.

> **"Learn to say 'no' to the good so you can say 'yes' to the best."**
> John C. Maxwell

CHAPTER THREE

Managing Your Ego

Let's begin by highlighting the life and accomplishments of one of the greatest leaders in American history.

Dwight David Eisenhower.

Born in the humble town of Denison, Texas, he was accepted into the U.S. Military Academy at West Point. From there he attained the status of a five-star General and was assigned the task of Supreme Commander of the Allied Forces in Europe.

It was Eisenhower who had the responsibility for planning and supervising the successful invasion of France and Germany in 1944 also known as D-Day, the decisive battle on the beaches of Normandy that effectively ended Hitler's campaign to rule the world.

After the war, Eisenhower served as the Army Chief of Staff under President Harry Truman and in 1951, he was named the first supreme commander of NATO. As if he had not done enough already, he then assumed the position of President of Columbia University, an Ivy League school and one of the most prestigious colleges in the country.

Then, he became the 34th President of the United States of America.

An amazing man, and a confident leader.

He also had a great approach to the way he led others. Just as remarkable as all his accomplishments, was his refusal to become conceited or arrogant. Check out his words on humility:

"Humility must always be the portion of any man who receives acclaim earned in the blood of his followers and the sacrifices of his friends."

This giant of history accomplished more than 99% of anyone who ever lived. Yet, he never let his ego get in the way of the people who made him great. He gave the recognition to those who made it possible for him to succeed.

A great leader has a healthy ego. This is not an anomaly, this is an asset.

You have to believe in your dreams, goals, opinions, plans, and the way you live your life. You have to possess confidence in yourself.

But, not at the expense of manipulating others.

Like Eisenhower, use your inner strengths to empower others. If you have a strong ego, chances are you are dominant in any crowd, and can be a bit intimidating to those you work with, maybe even feared by those you lead.

It's not your position that defines you, it's the way you apply it to others.

> "The key to successful leadership today
> is influence, not authority."
> Kenneth Blanchard

This involves managing your ego, understanding it, appreciating it, respecting it, taming it and controlling it in several key areas of your life. Let's look at the key points on how to become great in life by remaining humble in your heart and actions:

Listen to others

One of the common mistakes you may make in conversation involves the use of your quick mind. Simply put, you may answer too quickly, many times before the other person has finished speaking. Why? Because you have already ascertained not only the direction they are going with their statement but your response to it.

SUGGESTION: Use the, "Seven Seconds of Silence," the classy stillness of truly listening. Set aside your ego for a moment and let them finish. It shows respect for them and their thoughts.

> "The word 'listen' contains the same letters as the word 'silent.' "
> Alfred Brendel

Wanting attention

Growing up, you may have been the class clown or, "the life of the party." If so, you are familiar with being the center of attention. That may be great for entertainment but not effective in leading others.

SUGGESTION: Learn to harness your personality to include and involve others in your aura, making them feel part of the center of attention too.

Success

You didn't become successful alone, you had plenty of help. Because of that, don't forget your roots and the people who got you there. That should sober your heady view of yourself and give you a texture of grace coated with gratitude.

One of my favorite examples of this comes from the late, great running back, Walter Payton. He is arguably the greatest ever, and had a wonderful career in the 1970's and 1980's with my beloved Chicago Bears.

Every time Walter scored – and he scored 115 touchdowns over 13 seasons – he didn't spike the ball and dance around so all the world could see his success. Instead, he would score and simply hand the ball to one of his lineman to spike the ball.

Walter's example of giving others the credit, sharing the glory, and remaining humble while achieving so much, is a great reminder to us all.

SUGGESTION: Use your strong sense of ego to consistently *serve others* in the same way others served you on the way up.

Sales

The success of any sale does not always depend on the sale but on the service to the potential buyer. You are in the solution finding and problem solving business, not just the sell at any cost business. If you ascertain that the customer does not need the product or cannot truly afford it, don't sell it to them. That's just as successful a sale than any contract you close.

This is where your ego has to be secure enough to let a sale pass by for the sake of the individual who needs you, and counts on you, to be trustworthy.

SUGGESTION: Post a note on your desk, "Customer First," and follow it faithfully. It's not always about the commission you make but the consideration for others in how you act.

Motivation

Your ego is vital in motivating others, since it *provides the confidence* they need to believe your passion and plan for them. People will follow you if you are a decisive leader and you have a successful manner about you.

SUGGESTION: Take that confident ego of yours and *list ways* you can motivate others in a caring and positive manner enriching their lives. There's nothing more rewarding than bringing a smile to the face of a person who needs it that day.

> "There is nothing more beautiful than someone who goes out of their way to make life beautiful for others."
> Mandy Hale

Professional perspective

A leader with a healthy ego wants others to succeed. Your gift to your co-workers, colleagues, clients and employees is to bring their ideas and creativity to the forefront. As you invite them to share in an environment of acceptance and enthusiasm for their contributions, you will see a wealth of knowledge and inventiveness emanating from them.

An insecure ego cannot handle the opinions, ideas and input from those around them. Open your doors and let their ideas freely flow and you will not only be a great leader, you will be a better person.

SUGGESTION: Create ways to reward them for their contributions including: "Employee of the Week," a weekly round table and interoffice recognition.

Attitude and choice

Managing your ego has to work in the attitudinal trenches. Your patience will be tested the most when people offend you. Your ego has to be controlled, calm, and respectful in those situations.

If you are anything like me, this may be an ongoing challenge for you.

If your boss is screaming at you or you have a very dissatisfied client, how will you respond? Can you, will you, remain positive in your response? It's our human nature that wants to defend or strike back at the accuser. Manage your ego here.

SUGGESTION: When someone raises their voice to you or goes on a rant, the most powerful way you can respond is to sit there and say nothing in return. Put some time between your stimulus and your response. Eventually, the verbal attacker will either calm down or cease talking, allowing the situation to begin a cooling off period and eventually become fruitful for progress.

Just remember the adage, "Hurt people, hurt people." If they are demeaning you they are most likely emotionally wounded and are lashing out at the world. Yelling back at them is not the way to handle them or the situation.

> **"Most people do not listen
> with the intent to understand;
> they listen with the intent to reply."**
> Stephen R. Covey

Hold off on replying by playing verbal "rope-a-dope" and let the one ranting pummel you until they tire themselves out. Then, you can gently respond. That's managing your ego to full effectiveness in attitude and choice, my friend.

The key to motivational leadership: Understanding and controlling your ego

What is your motivation to become a leader?

Are you seeking power and fame?

Or, are you caring about people and their potential?

Be honest with yourself and your motives here.

> **"Leadership is something you do
> *for* someone, not *to* someone."**

History is filled with examples of great people making catastrophic failures because they couldn't manage their egos. "The greater the talent the greater the fall" epitomized the tragic sagas of: Richard Nixon, Woody Hayes, George Armstrong Custer, O.J. Simpson, Rod Blagojevich and on and on.

These individuals were well-known but they sabotaged themselves from becoming great because they allowed the fame, power and glory to insulate them from reality.

Instead of having advisers to guide them with wisdom, they embarked on a self-destructive course of shame, their legacy forever tarnished.

The ego giveth and the ego taketh away.

It can make you or break you. Take control of it.

"Do you wish to rise? Begin by descending. You plan a tower that will pierce the clouds. Lay first the foundation of humility."
Saint Augustine

Practical steps to maintaining a healthy ego.

1. Identify your specific ego issue

   An insecure ego can be manifested in too much confidence or too little confidence. Both are ego-based and prideful. We always assume that egomaniacs are always bragging but they can also be constantly self-deprecating to a fault. If you are always putting yourself down, that's *also* an unhealthy ego.
   Other ego issues might show up as: arrogance, narcissism, a quick temper, addictive behavior, manipulating others, self-victimization, self-sabotage, meanness, an obsessive hunger for power, self-loathing, impulsive and rash decision-making, unnecessary stubbornness, dread and having to constantly control your situations.

2. Origin of your issue

   An unhealthy ego can begin at birth with your DNA tendencies but more likely will be caused by your childhood upbringing and environment, the fertile and sad soil of abuse, injustice, lack of love and nurturing, constant loss of personal control, ongoing anger or a growing feeling you are better or worse than others around you.

3. List examples of where & how it has hurt you

    Over the years our ego has gotten all of us in trouble. List the major times it has hurt you to see if you can spot a pattern of behavior that is slowly getting worse. "Information is power" here.

4. Stop the cycle

    Once you identify the source, development and texture of your ego issue make a decision to put an end to its destructive power over you.

5. Reverse your behavior

    Either with the aid of a therapist, your advisers or going at it alone, you need to realize when your behavior is inappropriate and refuse to allow it to stop you from reaching your dreams. Had Custer acted upon this truth, he wouldn't have rashly ridden into the valley of the Little Big Horn, Nixon would have served his full term as President, Rod Blagojevich wouldn't be in jail for trying to sell the senate seat, King David would have left Bathsheba alone and the leaders of Enron wouldn't have destroyed the company. You get the idea; there are countless other stories of self destruction.

6. Ego Buster: Unselfish deeds

    The best antidote for a feeling of superiority or inferiority is helping others in an ongoing, unselfish way. It not only benefits them and makes you feel better about yourself; it replaces the egotistical toxins with a soothing balm of a gracious spirit.

7. Ego Buster: Promote other

   Instead of always being the CEO or the celebrity who feeds on others to get ahead, be the publicist and promoter who delights in helping them succeed. There's no greater use of your ego than to make other people smile.

8. Ego Buster: Toast, don't boast

   Celebrate life with a constant salute to the victories of those around you. Use your personal power and confidence to bring altruism to the world, not just attention to yourself.

   My grandfather had this wisdom for me, he would say, "Son, no need to go and tell people how great you are by tooting your own horn, people will know how great you are by the quality of the music you make."

> "When we are high on our ego we are suffering from self-delusion, and self-delusion always leads to confusion and turmoil."
>
> Anil Sinha

Your ego is an ATV that can take you just about anywhere, over rocks, hills and bumpy roads. But, it's up to you to ensure it doesn't drive you off a cliff.

For those who allowed that to happen, they are tragic examples of a promising life gone bad.

For those who stayed within the limits of a healthy self-essence, they not only contributed to the world in wondrous ways, they enjoyed the experience of a life worth living.

> **"Humility is not thinking less of yourself, it's thinking of yourself less."**
>
> C.S. Lewis

CHAPTER FOUR

Honing Your Skills

There once was a young man from Illinois whose dream was to be a lumberjack. He set out across the country to the Northwest to find himself a new life. After days of driving, he finally made it. He arrived at the work site and walked into the foreman's office. He announced, "My name is Brad and I want to be a lumberjack."

The foreman looked at the tall, thin, young man and explained, "Son, this ain't for the meek or mild at heart, this here is work. Are you ready to put in long days, rain or shine, and literally work your fingers to the bone?"

"Yes sir, I am!" exclaimed Brad.

He was hired on the spot.

The next day he arrived right on time at 7:00am. Brad was determined to be a great lumberjack.

He worked eight straight hours, non-stop, with sweat constantly pouring down his face. He loved his new job. He was a lumberjack. At the end of the day, when all the employees turned in their counts, Brad excitedly waited at the end of the line.

One by one, the men recorded their tree cutting numbers, twelve, ten, fifteen, eleven...it was now his turn.

Brad walked up and turned in his number of tree falls of *twenty-one!* No one could believe it. Not only did he have the best count that day, it was a new company record surpassing the previous figure by two trees.

Brad was elated.

The next morning the young lumberjack couldn't wait to get up and start chopping down trees. He rose early and began his shift with a promise to himself, "I'm going to beat my own record!"

But, as the day wore on, Brad was very tired. Unlike the first day, he had to take some breaks to rest. When his shift ended, he had cut down seventeen trees, a good number, but it wasn't a record.

Nonetheless, he wouldn't let a slower day stop him, so he got to bed early and prepared for another day. For the next several days, he worked longer hours, up to sixteen per day. He ended up with blisters on his fingers and hands.

He was so tired he could barely stand up to work. Brad was still cutting down trees, about ten per day, which was average, but he was frustrated.

He felt he had failed as a lumberjack.

So, after two weeks of declining productivity, Brad slowly made his way into the foreman's office and sighed, "I quit."

The foreman was shocked.

"Why would you quit?" asked his boss.

Brad whimpered, "I'm so tired. I'm cutting down half the trees since my record day and I'm working almost double the time. This isn't working. I'm no good at this. I need to quit."

In frustration, he threw his axe on the foreman's desk.

The foreman examined the axe and smiled. "Brad, I'm surprised you were able to cut down even one tree with this axe, let alone ten. This might be the dullest axe I have ever seen. When was the last time you sharpened this thing?"

A shocked Brad didn't know he needed to sharpen his axe at all. He hadn't sharpened it once when it should have been sharpened every day. The problem wasn't his effort, it was his effectiveness.

His great skill was not enough to maintain excellence. He needed to hone his axe in order to stay at his high level of execution.

HONE: def. to sharpen or to make more acute, intense, or effective.

When was the last time you honed your skills?

If your axe is dull, it's time for you to sharpen it.

There are three practical levels of honing your skills.

LEVEL ONE: Education and Effort

1. Learn your level of expertise

   Make a promise to yourself to be the best in your workplace at what you do. Whether you are a sales rep, a teacher, a marketing consultant, a bus driver, a soccer mom, a pastor, a nurse, a farmer or a C-suite executive, be your best. Don't settle for average, go for the top. At the very least, work harder than anyone at your position so that you are the most knowledgeable in the field. Most organizations don't train their employees effectively. If you train yourself, you are way ahead of the game.

2. Master new technology

   As well as you may understand the computer, social media and other technologies today, you can always get better. Technology is the most effective tool you have at your fingertips. The computer and all the advancements can make your skills come alive in dozens of ways. The more you master it, the more you will excel at your job.

3. Read, read, read!

   If information is power, become more powerful. Read everything in your field: from marketing reports to industry articles, from creative ways others have succeeded in doing their jobs to biographies of great men and women in your line of work. Did I say "read?" Read, read, read!

   Level One is about gathering information. Subscribe to several publications and devour them. Learn from any expert there is to hone your craft. It will cost you a little extra money each month, but it will pay off in spades as you absorb all the material.

   Don't just read it, highlight it, set up a new file, and label it, "Honing my Axe." Set up a note page on your tablet or smart phone and summarize what you are reading. When you retype it, you will learn the information a second time and sear it into your memory.

> **"If I had eight hours to chop down a tree, I'd spend six hours sharpening my axe."**
> Abraham Lincoln

A college student attending a conference in Southern California heard a motivational speaker and was impressed enough to approach him after the dynamic presentation to ask the charismatic leader for advice.

"Mr. McDowell," he queried, "I want to be a great speaker like you. What advice can you give me?"

The man looked at him and said one word, "Speak."

Then, he turned and walked away leaving the student standing there.

Great advice.

The best way to be good at something is to excel at it by experiencing it over and over again. You've gathered the data, now apply it...

 "There's no substitute for experience."

LEVEL TWO: Get *to* it

1. The best education is to experience it

    How does a mechanic become an expert on cars? He works on them. He works on all types, makes and models, and not for a few days or a week, but for a lifetime. Let me share a motto I saw painted on the side of a semi while traveling on the interstate, "The road to success does not have shortcuts."

2. Skills are not honed in theory, but in practice

    It's like waking up in the morning. You lay there conscious and alert with all the plans you have for the day but until you get out of bed, you are immersed in intellect and not embodied in exercise. You are not judged on your ideas but the implementation of them. Put one foot on the floor, add the other one and get moving. That's not dreaming it, it's doing it!

Dreams are good. Goals are good to. But you must ACT, why? Here is an acronym to help:

Action Changes Things

Go out and do something, ACT today!

3. Imagination without execution is unavailing

It's not what you dream, it's what you do. Chart your course but don't forget your "tennies." No one ever threw a game winning touchdown pass from the huddle. A great quote for you to memorize from James Russell Lowell, "All the beautiful sentiments in the world weigh less than a single, lovely action."

LEVEL THREE: Sharpening the Axe

1. Hone your skills at any age

At the beginning of your career, you hone to become good at what you do. In the middle of your career, you hone to be the best. In the twilight of your career, you hone to adjust your expertise much like a pitcher who develops a slider because he has lost the speed on his fast ball. Keep adapting as you grow not just to survive, but to succeed. If you need to go back to school or attend a leadership seminar to make your axe sharper, so be it. As noted in my first book, *Soul on Fire*, a leader is always improving.

2. Record yourself

    Athletes and entertainers are constantly evaluating themselves by watching video of their performance. That's how they adjust their skills and improve on them. Examine yourself doing a sales pitch, making a motivational speech, guiding a panel discussion or pushing your marketing plan to your co-workers. You may spot some things you can do more effectively.

    REMEMBER THIS: *the tape doesn't lie.* Watch. Be honest. Adjust. You *will* get better. "It's what we learn after we know it all that counts!"

3. Hire a trainer to be your expert

    Ask co-workers, friends, and those around you to give you an honest 360 degree review. Make your axe sharper and more productive. Let a professional give you the input you need to grow and improve.

They say, "You can't teach an old dog new tricks." Yes, you can! If you are in the later years of your career, learn to be a young dog again. Keep getting better as you grow older.

In over 25 years as basketball official I have seen over 1,000 games live, not including all those I watched on TV. The score at the half matters *none!* The score with five minutes left in the game matters not.

In close games the team that finishes strong usually wins. You may be in the 4th quarter of your life, but your life isn't over…so finish strong!

The world is changing *rapidly*. If you aren't honing skills you will be swallowed up in a heartbeat. You need to learn new methods, new ways, new technology, new tactics, new information, new packaging and new strategies.

New, new, new!

> "No matter how much experience you have,
> how many degrees you have,
> or how well known you have become –
> there is always something new to learn.
> Don't rest on your past experiences.
> If you do nothing to improve your skills,
> you won't stay where you are."
> Laura Spencer

The more years you put in, the more your axe needs to be sharpened. Why should only the young professionals be hungry to be the best? If you are passionate about your job, your age should never be an issue. An eagle is an eagle is an eagle. Keep soaring over new mountains.

Honing your skills and learning new ones is a remarkable journey. Reinventing yourself and revitalizing skills you mastered years ago is a career epiphany that will thrill your soul and enhance your professional value.

> "There is a difference between skill and talent.
> Master the skill to allow the talent out."
> Ziad K. Abdelnour

Clint Eastwood and Ron Howard became Academy Award winning directors to extend their careers as their acting days were winding down. George Blanda was an all-pro quarterback who aged nicely into a full-time place kicker and won the prestigious Bert Bell Award in 1970. When Muhammad Ali lost his knockout punch, he learned how to "rope-a-dope," a defensive tactic of being hit constantly on the ropes to win the heavyweight championship of the world in 1974.

New skills, new approaches, new techniques and new successes are hallmarks of the consummate professional. Learn to walk down the darkened hallway of life and find the sliver of radiance, which reveals new vistas of opportunities, to become great again.

"What a profoundly satisfying feeling when one finally gets on top of a new set of skills and then sees the light under the new door those skills can open, even as another door is closing."
Gail Sheehy

"It's not how hard you work or how much time you put in, it's how *effective* you work."

You have your trusty ax. You don't need a new one. Just rework the blade to continue to be the best you can be until you are ready to hang it up.

Until then, keep getting better. We need you. You still have a lot to offer with the skills and talent you have at your disposal.

The world is waiting for you.

CHAPTER FIVE

Your Work Ethic

Do most people get what they want? Not unless they want it badly enough.

Do most people get what they deserve? Depends greatly on their work ethic.

WORK ETHIC: def. a set of values based on the moral virtues of hard work and diligence.

Reaching your dreams isn't just about talent or luck. It comes down to something more basic than those gifts.

Breaking the hard ground through good old-fashioned sweat.

Let me tell you a story about my niece and her work ethic.

When she was a senior in high school she had decided to go to college to become a nurse. She was caring, loving, intelligent and social. She had all the attributes to be a great nurse.

She was accepted into two colleges that had nursing schools, but they were not equal when it came to her intended major.

One had a better program than the other.

My niece wanted the advanced level of nursing excellence at *that* school.

But, the higher rated school had a policy that they do not accept incoming freshman into the nursing program. She would have to study there as an underclassman for one year, achieve an excellent GPA, and then apply for the nursing program in her sophomore year.

The spots were limited, so only about half of the sophomores get accepted. Most of the others either change majors or transfer to a new school.

She wanted to be a nurse. She wanted to be in *that* program. She needed to do more and go beyond the normal effort and work to achieve it. This is where her strong work ethic kicked in.

She retook her ACT and raised her score three points, up to a 29. Just two weeks later the top-notch program sent her a letter and welcomed her directly into their prestigious nursing program as a freshman!

This was not normally what they do for first year students, but they did it for her.

Because of her extra effort, she received higher results. The status quo was a standard to accept things as they are, but to do that, she was in jeopardy of losing her dream. Instead, "she walked the wall until she found the door."

That *wall* was sacrifice and work, and it paid off.

A strong work ethic usually does.

"We do what we have to so we can do what we want to."
James Farmer

A great work ethic can be summarized in three practical segments: Beginning, Middle and End, just like a movie script.

Except, your life is far more serious. It is real. It is who you are and what you accomplish.

Beginning – It's all about *attitude*

The first practical step of a strong work ethic is your attitude. Every morning, when you first wake up you have to tell yourself, "If I'm going to be effective today, I must choose to have the right attitude about my work, and my life."

You are deciding to be positive about your labor, not fearful, not lazy, not cynical and not reluctant. *Stay positive*. If you don't have that commitment I have a suggestion for you.

Go back to bed.

Stay there until you are ready to fight for the values of your life.

The will to do it and the positive attitude to work hard is like a shield protecting you from being frustrated and negative going to battle. Put on your armor just like a warrior heading to the front line.

This is not wanderlust. This is war.

It's time for you to focus. It's time for you to fight. It's time for you to make your mark on the world. Let your legacy begin.

Start the day with something that puts you in a positive frame of mind for battle. Your early morning steps are critical to your daily achievements.

A workout
A good run or fast walk
Meditation
Spiritual inspiration
A good breakfast

Get to work early so you can prepare your paperwork, plans and files for the day. Avoid any interaction with events or people that tend to depress or discourage you. You need that positive momentum right now.

My good friend Steve Reitsch has a phrase that sums up the attitude we need each day, and the type of people we need to surround ourselves with:

"No time for stinkin' thinkin'!"

Middle – Be excellent

Leaders with a healthy work ethic don't work to just get through the day, or simply survive in life, they work to excel. Their principle of work ethic and the people they work with, work for and lead, is all about excellence, never the status quo.

"Excellence in everything, and in everything, excellence."

Here is a practical plan of attitudes to build a great work day.

Approach your work with these action words that typify your work ethic philosophy:

Creative

Bold

Fearless

Persistent

Imaginative

Tough

Resourceful

Throughout your day, I want you to walk away from the status quo, deviate from the norm, take risks, never procrastinate, follow through, add a dash of imagination to everything you do, always figure out a solution to any obstacles and be a warrior, not letting anyone or anything discourage you from your mission.

Do you hear me, Spartacus?

Be my gladiator.

> **"Build a good name.**
> **Keep your name clean.**
> **Don't make compromises, don't worry about making a bunch of money or being successful –**
> **be concerned with doing good work**
> **and make the right choices and protect your work.**
> **And, if you build a good name, eventually,**
> **that name will be its own currency."**
> William S. Burroughs

There are students in high school and college who are happy with a C-, just enough to pass a class or graduate. That doesn't cut it in the adult world. This isn't Algebra or French class. This is your life!

You need to be a straight "A" student, NOW. And in every single moment moving forward.

End – finish well

It's time to complete your work day with the right ethics to make it successful, both in character and competitiveness. Challenge yourself with these four questions before you head for home. Don't let up now.

Are there any projects, paperwork or presentations I missed?

Did I give every bit of my work the best I had today?

Did I take any selfish shortcuts?

Is there something I need to go back and improve before I leave?

These questions make the difference between mediocrity and excellence. If you need to clean up a file or improve something, don't wait, do it. As Vince Lombardi said, "You don't do things right most of the time, you do them right all of the time."

The ending of your workday, week and life should be as strong, or stronger than your beginning and middle. A champion always fights to the very last second.

That's why he or she is a champion.

> "It was character that got us out of bed, commitment that moved us into action, and discipline that enabled us to follow through."
> Zig Ziglar

When I was in high school, one of my buddies and I was offered a lawn job, which involved hard work with a fairly good payment. When I went to pick up my friend to ride over to do the yard work, his dad opened the door and was unaware of our Saturday morning chore.

"My son is still asleep," he informed me. "I don't think he'll be joining you at work today." I was surprised at my friend's laziness, yet I went ahead and did the work without him.

When I saw my friend at school, he said that he was "just too tired" to do the work. I was shocked. As high school students, we always needed money, and beyond that, we made a commitment to be there for the elderly widow.

My grandfather was aware of the incident and he had a take on it. "This isn't the kind of friend you need in your life, Randy. He's not a hard worker, he's a slacker. You need to surround yourself with people who take their job seriously and have a great work ethic. Or, you will become lazy just like them."

He was right.

> "Some say if you want success surround yourself with successful people.
> I say if you want true and lasting success surround yourself with people of integrity."
> Charles Glassman

A strong work ethic isn't just about labor; it's about character, integrity, sacrifice and personal responsibility. It's the stuff of leaders.

It's my hope you work harder and happier than anyone you know. That you become great in the workplace, and in the ethical place. Make the world better because you're working in it.

Get to work.

Make a difference.

Be excellent in everything you do.

CHAPTER SIX

Advisers

> "The trouble with good advice
> is that it usually interferes with our plans."
> Croft M. Pentz

Every successful career person needs great advisers around him or her. This is easier said than done. Most great advice is usually after the wrong decision has been made, after the damage has been done.

Examples of this abound in history.

We all know now that General George Armstrong Custer and his 7th Calvary should never have been led by his large ego into Little Bighorn that day. It's pretty obvious to all of us after the fact.

The Titanic should have focused on icebergs floating dangerously in the Atlantic Ocean instead of trying to set a speed record from England to the United States.

President Nixon should have been surrounded by great advisers who would have counseled him to not lie about what he knew about Watergate; instead he was surrounded by advisers who were either insulating him from moral reality or "yes men" who were afraid to point him toward it.

> "Great advisers can guide you to a great career, poor counsel can destroy it."

> "The best advisers, helpers and friends, always are not those who tell us how to act in special cases, but who give us out of themselves, the ardent spirit and desire to act right."
> Phillip Brooks

When it comes to making sound decisions we need to paraphrase John Donne, "No man should be an island."

What will stop you from setting up great advisers in your life?

The first barrier is you.

Many of us have large egos and we don't ask or take advice well from others. As Joseph Addison accurately dissected human nature in this area, "There is nothing which we receive with so much reluctance as advice."

Ultimately, you need to make the final decision. Sure. But, it will behoove you to allow others the input to give you all the aspects, good or bad, of that decision.

You have to have a healthy ego to be decisive in the end but not arrogant enough to believe you don't need counsel in reaching that point.

> "Don't follow any advice, no matter how good, until you feel as deeply in your spirit as you think in your mind that the counsel is wise."
> Joan Rivers

The second barrier is your need for privacy.

I am with you on this one. No one is recommending you seek the public counsel of 350 people on Facebook here!

We all have fear of someone seeing us fail. We don't want to be exposed for being in need, or asking for help. We don't want to be a burden. In short, we protect ourselves.

The best people are those that can look in the mirror and be honest. I am in my mid, well I guess late forties, and when I look in the mirror I do not see the young man I was twenty years ago. I cannot escape the fact, aging is visible.

You need to take the same approach to your decisions and actions in life. Take out a mirror, allow others to look in and speak into your life. They aren't there to judge, they are there because they love you and want to help you.

Let those few people in that you trust to have discretion and give honest advice.

And the third barrier is fear of being wrong.

You may not solicit advice because you may be concerned someone will mislead you, or the advice may not work out as planned. There are various fears we as humans dread and one of them is the fear of being wrong.

We would rather make no decision than make an unintelligent one. If that is to be the case, we may prefer to make it on our own with no input from another.

"No enemy is worse than bad advice." Sophocles

But, the overwhelming truth is that you will benefit from great advice. So, here's the how-to list of what to look for in your counsel.

Advisers should have several assets in order to be invaluable for you, they are:

High morals

A great adviser should have a strong sense of right and wrong and committed to the truth of what needs to be done in a situation. The quality of character in the one giving you advice is non-negotiable for a long-term positive outcome.

Cares for you

You need an individual who is committed to you and always wants the best for you. Without that belief in you, you are in danger of being manipulated by the adviser. You want someone that will tell you what you need to hear not what you want to hear.

Wisdom

As you may know, wisdom is different from intelligence. Wisdom is the ability to think and act utilizing knowledge, experience, understanding, common sense, and insight, a combination of factors to safeguard you.

Expertise

It is recommended that you have several advisers in each field of your concern. Your sibling can give you insight into a family issue but they may not be the best adviser for a career step. A co-worker could help you make a decision on a work project but not in choosing the right spouse for you.

Experience

Don't follow the lead of someone who talks their opinion; listen to the one who has walked their opinion.

"The quality of any advice
anybody has to offer has to be judged
against the quality of life they actually lead."

Douglas Adams

Choosing your adviser team is a skilled art. An example of this brilliance is found in the career of John Fitzgerald Kennedy. Here is a blueprint for adviser circles success.

Outer circle

Over the years of his political career, JFK chose and discarded hundreds of advisers who could take him to each level. As he arrived there, he stripped off the mentors who could not go to the next plateau with him. This demonstrated the truth, "some mentors are for a lifetime and some are for a season."

Specialty circle

JFK had advisers for his speech writing, political campaign runs, social networks, legal issues and brain trust, all invaluable in their area of expertise for him.

Cabinet circle

It's been stated that President Kennedy had the finest Cabinet of any chief executive in history.

When you examine closely the people he surrounded himself with, they are awe-inspiring in their intellectual brilliance, competence, experience, ability to solve issues and reputation.

Close adviser circle

A small cavalcade of superstars including, Theodore Sorenson, Richard Goodwin, Arthur Schlesinger and Lawrence O'Brien.

Inner circle

JFK trusted two individuals more than anyone in the world, his father Joseph P. Kennedy and his brother, Robert. They were the men who helped him win every political race he entered and guided him through the crises of the Democratic primaries (he won all seven he entered), the potentially crippling steel strike, civil rights, dealing with Nikita Khrushchev over the Berlin wall and the Nuclear Test Ban Treaty and, of course, the Cuban Missile Crisis.

I advise you to set up several circles of friends, specialists, career mentors and family members. Create your wall, a backyard fence that will always protect your personal and professional house from being robbed, vandalized or burned down.

Advisers serve as that wall around you. The stronger and layered the wall is with quality material, the safer you will be in your decision-making.

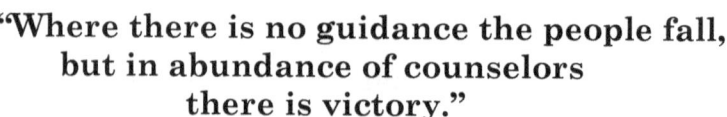

> "Where there is no guidance the people fall, but in abundance of counselors there is victory."
> Proverbs 11:14

I have a career circle for FoxPoint, a basketball circle, a creative circle, an accountability circle, and an inner circle. This last one is comprised of my wife, my brother and my mom; the three people who know me best and love me the most.

My wife, Marne, is special. She epitomizes the truth of a wife with character, love for me, and wisdom.

> **"Let no man under value the price of a virtuous woman's counsel."**
> George Chapman

I am not only in love with her, she is my best friend, the person I admire most and my most trusted adviser.

Keep that in mind when you choose your spouse. A great one is indispensable for your personal and professional life.

Advisers.

They can make you or break you.

With them, Custer would have stayed out of Montana, the Titanic would have made a slower and safer arrival to New York and President Nixon would have completed his second term and been considered one of the greatest Presidents in history for all his accomplishments.

But, because of an absence of counsel, history unfolded in a far different way.

I personally believe in advisers with one good reason.

I was twenty-three years old. The excitement and challenge of graduating college and beginning my life and career was upon me. I had multiple job offers to choose from and an important life decision to make.

I needed advice.

Following my parent's divorce, my mom had always encouraged me to trust older men as role models with experience and wisdom. My dad was distant, so I reached out to someone who had always been there for me in critical moments.

I turned to my Uncle Jim.

He was the man to help solve one of the biggest decisions of my young life.

I shared with him that I had narrowed my choices between two positions, at two very different companies.

One was to be in sales for the fourth largest printing company in the United States, the other was to sell for a small printer in southern Illinois. The former would place me in a fantastic training ground and I would be part of a half billion dollar company with many divisions and options.

The latter would make me their point man to lead their small team into the Chicago area market for the first time.

> **"Never let the best
> be the enemy of the good."**
> Voltaire

As with many things in life, both companies and decisions were good, but one was *best*. As a young professional it was vital to make the best decision.

My Uncle Jim was the man here. He had 30 years of experience as a leader and a manager. He cared for me personally. I trusted him. He was the perfect adviser for my life at that point in time.

Instead of telling me what to do, he walked me through a series of questions. He gave me an exercise that would help me prioritize what was important to me, challenging me to determine the pros and cons for each position.

He wanted me to ultimately decide which career was my heart and talent.

I chose the larger company. Most importantly, I made the final decision, which is exactly what my uncle had guided me to do. That is a great adviser, not telling you what to decide but opening the way for you to tell *yourself*.

Soon after I began work, I found my talents were better in a different position and because they were a large company, I was able to find my perfect niche there.

As the years went by, I kept an eye on the other company to see when they would break into the Chicago area. They never did. They were always too small to pull it off.

I had made the right decision, thanks to my wise uncle.

Go find your wise men and women; they're out there waiting for you.

> **"The fellowship of true friends
> who can hear you out,
> share your joys,
> help carry your burdens,
> and correctly counsel you is priceless."**
> Ezra Taft Benson

CHAPTER SEVEN

Using Failure to Succeed

Failure.

A word that strikes fear in any aspect of our life.

Failure.

A concept that prevents many of us from believing we can accomplish something.

Failure.

A criticism that has the power to stay with us for years and years.

We all know its negative force in our world; now let's do something about it as a leader. Let's harness its' dynamic to launch us all the way to our Dream.

> "The positive way you handle failure and make it your friend will be the ultimate key to your success."

There are *three truths* of failure that we will address:

1. **Most failure is the result of poor decision-making,** *not* **the failure itself.**

The simplest way to define failure is to identify it as, "falling short." But, that is not the whole truth. We have to address the root question, "falling short of what?"

Most failures in our lives are a result of a misguided goal or practice at their point of origin. The failure that occurs as a result of a poor choice is not the problem; it is that the goal was wrong to begin with.

Think of a girl or guy you dated in the past and how she or he was not the right person for you. The relationship ended because your love for each other "fell short."

Did it?

No, that wasn't the problem. You didn't fail. You actually succeeded by shedding the dysfunctional relationship.

The failure was actually a success.

Another example, you got fired from a job you were ill-suited for in the first place. It wasn't your specialty, talent or passion.

Did you fail?

Not at all, you succeeded by failing at a career that didn't fit you.

"What seem to us as bitter trials are often blessings in disguise."
Oscar Wilde

Failure in these examples is like a career or a relationship lie detector test.

Failure forces you to tell the truth to yourself about who you are, what you should be doing with your talents and priorities, and making the changes necessary to correct the problem.

If you don't do it, failure will. That is a good thing. Failure in this light is not being a failure at all.

A vital how-to for you. If you are struggling in an area of your career or with a personal relationship or hobby, jot it down and ask yourself:

"Am I failing here because I am not good enough or because I should never have taken this on in the first place?"

If it's the latter, eliminate it and focus on what you do best.

Let's move on to a second truth about the failure process.

2. Failure is not the opposite of success; the opposite of both is not trying.

People are afraid to fail. That shouldn't be their main fear. The thing that should terrorize them is never trying something in the first place.

What if the Wright brothers never tried? We would be taking buses everywhere to this day. What if Edison had not invented the light bulb? Enjoy walking around the dark banging your shins into the coffee table, do you?

> "Winners are not afraid of losing. But losers are. Failure is part of the process of success. People who avoid failure also avoid success."
> Robert T. Kiyosaki, Rich Dad, Poor Dad

Look around the room right now, or maybe even in your hand. What do you think of all those conveniences at your fingertips? They were created, built, modified and polished with failure before they got to your home.

I think of men and women who kept trying until they failed enough to finally succeed.

I think of Norm Larson and his team of product developers who spent countless hours, and dollars, working on their goal. They failed over and over again. I am sure the team was frustrated, and the finance team gave them tremendous pressure to succeed. No different than your life today.

We know they eventually succeeded. What they *didn't* know at the time was how many failures they would need to overcome. In the end, they failed 39 times before they made it to the promised land, and gave us WD 40!

Trying is not the goal. Neither is being afraid to try. There's only one way to succeed.

> "Get busy living or get busy dying."
> Andy Dufresne

Here is the epitaph of a sad life:

> "Never won, never lost, never tried.
> This person just existed."

Life is too short to let your fear prevent you from reaching your Dream. The fear may protect you from failing, but the fear also prevents you from succeeding.

It is a double-edged sword. Learn to make it a single-edged sword.

Get out there and start taking control of your fears instead of letting them take control of you.

A great way to do that is to use "The Lion's Roar" concept in your war against your fears. The most feared animal in the jungle is the male lion, but the truth is that he is not the main predator within his own family.

In most cases, he is old, toothless and does not possess the power to run.

The main hunters are the lionesses that lurk in the brush for vulnerable prey. It is the job of the male lion to roar, scaring the gazelle, wildebeest or antelope into the area where the female lionesses are waiting for them.

The females kill them and as they begin to eat their victims the male lion lopes over and joins them. His teeth and savagery are nowhere near the quality of his female counterparts.

His gift is the roar.

In order to survive, "The Lion's Roar," you must run towards it, not away from it.

It's the same with your fears. Run at them, not away from them. They are not potent when you meet them head on. They are only powerful when you imagine their strength, rarely in reality.

3. You need a plan

A great statement for your leadership and for having personal power on your life:

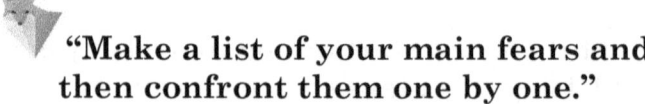

> "Make a list of your main fears and then confront them one by one."

Here are the steps to taming failure:

Promise yourself in advance you will learn from this risky venture

From the very beginning, you need to see the learned lessons, whether the result be good or bad. If you can accept that from the beginning, you will have a successful experience.

Have the courage to make the decision to try

You can't score unless you're on the playing field. Get out there and become a competitor.

Remain positive no matter what occurs

Keep your spirits up. As F. Scott Fitzgerald said, "Never confuse a single defeat with a final defeat." Of course, you will have setbacks. Expect them. Embrace them. Show them you are still the boss of them.

Keep seeing the big picture

Some people give up because they may see a crack in the sidewalk and lose sight of the horizon. Stay focused on your Dream. Don't let a chink in concrete ever take that beautiful sunset away from you.

Success does not come quickly

Focus on your daily effort, not on your ultimate result. Keep working steadily and steadfastly. Plod, plod, plod. Every day, give your best effort and eventually, the wall of impossibility will come crashing down and you will have your victory. One step at a time, Mr. Tortoise.

> "When I face the desolate impossibility
> of writing five hundred pages,
> a sick sense of failure falls on me,
> and I know I can never do it.
> Then gradually, I write one page
> and then another.
> One day's work is all I can
> permit myself to contemplate."
> John Steinbeck, Travels with Charley: In Search of America

Stay rested

Fatigue, poor eating habits and stress can wear you out. Don't let that happen to you. Take time to get away from your work and rest. Don't schedule yourself into depression. Close your eyes. Take a power nap. Enjoy an extended vacation. Refresh yourself and then hit it again when you have the energy to be great.

Reflection

This is a huge part of following your goal. Shut everything off, computer, sounds, noise, everything. Sit there with your eyes closed and reflect on what you are doing. Visualize your final result. Smile. Feel it. Let it come to you.

When

You *are* going to get there, that is not the issue. Be a "when" person. To a leader it is never "if," it is always *"when."* No one will stop you and you will not stop yourself. Keep going, keep going, keep going. You're almost there.

Make an updated list of your progress every 3–4 days to encourage yourself that you're moving ahead and distancing yourself from the past.

> **"The past is supposed to be a place of reference, not a place of residence!
> There is a reason why your car has a big windshield and a small rear view mirror.
> You are supposed to keep your eyes on where you are going, and just occasionally check out where you have been."**
> Willie Jolley

When it comes to failure and success, always be true to the three W's:

Willing to fail

Willing to gut it out no matter what

Willing to try again when you fall

A practical corporate idea:

Many years ago I had a client that was worth nearly 20% of our total sales. Needless to say, learning from, and using our failures for success, was paramount. At the end of each year, we collaborated on a "Lessons Learned" meeting.

It was not a recap of the progress made over the year. It was the lessons we needed to learn from that year to make further progress.

Some things we learned because they were a success and some because they were a failure. We asked ourselves, "What do we need to do differently?"

It wasn't, "You failed, you cost us and you're fired." It was to ensure that a strategy that fell short would not be put back on the board again. We learned from what worked, and we learned from what didn't.

Here is a suggestion, do the same thing with all your work this past year. Put up your professional "Lessons Learned" list and evaluate them. This should be a positive exercise intended to encourage your progress and modify your performance for the new year.

"Failure should be our teacher, not our undertaker. Failure is delay, not defeat. It is a temporary detour, not a dead end. Failure is something we can avoid only by saying nothing, doing nothing, and being nothing." Denis Waitley

A personal story on failure...leading to success.

I was graduating from college with multiple job offers in my field. I was about to get married. I was on top of the world.

After the honeymoon and we moved everything in, I began my corporate career selling commercial printing for the fourth largest printing company in the country. I completed my training and was ready to head out.

I pounded the pavement the old fashioned way, door

to door. Walking in, asking for people to meet with me or at least get a phone number.

Would you believe it? On day one, on call number one, I sold my first printing job. I was a salesman!

My quota was $100,000 in sales for year one. My first sale toward my quota was worth just $85. That wasn't my commission that was my sale. But I was excited.

From that point on, I thought that every call should have been a sale. When that didn't happen, I got frustrated. I did sell some more, but nothing close to my quota.

I remember the day my manager came to me and said, "Randy, we think we know what the problem is. You are very knowledgeable, professional and personable. When we play basketball as an office each week, you are very aggressive and competitive on the court, in a great way. What we don't see is that same personality as a sales rep."

Typically, when this conversation happened, the rep was let go. To be honest, I should have been fired. In my first year I sold $32,000. Translated, that's only 32% of my quota.

Not good.

Thankfully, my manager was a wise man. He offered me a position as a customer service manager. He recognized I wasn't fit for sales at that time.

Now I was at a crossroads in my career. I felt I had come short as a salesman. I could wallow in my failure and walk away in shame, or look at this as the beginning of a new career. I chose the latter.

I realized that I didn't have all the answers.

Failure had become my friend.

Failure revealed to me a new direction, and I threw myself into my new job, with everything I had.

I started listening to mentors and managers. Now, I had a whole new approach to my work, not expecting instant gratification, but steady progress. I took this new opportunity as a second chance, one to be fully experienced and appreciated.

I *could* do this. I *would* do this.

"If you fell down yesterday, stand up today."
H.G. Wells

I spent the next ten years with that corporation, and what a great ride it was!

I was promoted six times and ultimately came to the position of Plant Manager, responsible for the work of 150 people and a $35 million operation.

Failure? Nope. Just a crack in the sidewalk.

**"You're not obligated to win.
You're obligated to keep trying."**
Jason Mraz

By keeping my eye on the horizon, I was able to finally succeed at work. I learned from my past and moved ahead, on a journey filled with success.

I wish you the same.

Enjoy your learning experiences, and keep your eyes on the horizon.

Allow failure to be your friend.

Allow yourself to be *Refined by Fire*.

EPILOGUE

After I wrote my first book, **Soul on Fire,** on the passions of great leaders, I believed there needed to be a companion book to spell out many of the how-to methods for realizing those passions of leadership.

And, **Refined by Fire** was born.

This has been a rewarding book to write because it not only exhorts us to greatness but it explains the ways to get there. Inspiration without explanation usually leads to frustration.

I was committed to providing the practical applications of excellence.

I believe the world needs leaders like you and me. We can impact it not because of our title or position, but by our talents, passion and influence. We can improve on the past, empower the present and provide greatness for the future. We can be authentic.

Thank you for being part of this mission to be challenged by the fire, to endure it, and to come out the other side refined by it. I appreciate you.

To remind you of the quote that began this book,

Epilogue

> "Look around you.
> Everything changes.
> Everything on this earth is in a
> continuous state of evolving,
> refining, improving, adapting,
> enhancing...changing.
> You were not put on this earth to remain stagnant."
> Steve Maraboli

It still rings true. We have so much to do.

Keep growing.

Keep going.

The world is waiting for you!

Randy Fox

Randy

November 29, 2016

NOTES

NOTES

NOTES

NOTES

Epilogue

ACKNOWLEDGMENTS

As I journey forward in life, meaning I am getting older, and as I strive to change the world through my leadership message, I continue to realize how many people have influenced me. There are so many names that could be, and should be, mentioned here, yet in a collective shout, I say "thank you" to each person that has touched my life.

With a heart full of thanks and gratitude:

Marne, for your support, your love, and your guidance to help make this dream come true is beyond words.

To my close friends, the men in my life, I have spent many years with each of you. Each of you has a place at my table, always. Each of you has refined who I am. I love you guys, Steve Kodidek, Jeff Mikyska, Mike Taylor, Dave DeRousse, and Travis Dodge.

To all the leaders, managers and mentors that have taught me, led me, advised me, in particular:

Bill Cwinski, for teaching me how to mop a floor and to be proud doing it

Mark Fackler, for how to be in command yet always remain humble

Mike Schermer, for Tuesdays at 10

Tony Haugen, for a chance to sell, for second chances, and priorities that matter

Doug Lazzerini, for seeing that results do matter

Patty Broderick, for understanding, time and confidence in me

Al Raya and Don Baumgart, for the opportunity to grow

Steve McGrath, for dreaming, "prrrp"

Randy Tate, for a refining moment at Harvest

Pat Hurley, for all your words and guidance

To my mom, for your countless hours of editing, standing at ballparks and continual sacrifice.

Randy Fox

Speaker • Author

Turning Everyday People Into Superstar Leaders!

Standard presentations and workshops are great...
yet we recognize that your situation, your group,
your objectives are specific and unique to you...
and we think your event should be too!

Randy is happy to customize a presentation, seminar or workshop to match up perfectly with your needs.

To connect with Randy and learn more about FoxPoint, visit:

http://foxpoint.net

facebook.com/foxpoint

twitter.com/randy_foxpoint

linkedin.com/in/foxrandy

877.411.8498

You have a dream. You want to succeed. Find your passion and uncover the power and purpose of leadership. Live with a *Soul on Fire*.

Order your copy today!
http://foxpoint.net

The world is starving for real, authentic leaders to rise up and lead the world. We need trustworthy, honest, competent men and women to provide jobs, support, care for neighbors, employees and our world. This journey starts with you...be a leader worth following!

www.ingramcontent.com/pod-product-compliance
Lightning Source LLC
Chambersburg PA
CBHW032131090426
42743CB00007B/557